Beyond the Cloister

The Story of Nuns

Beyond the Cloister: The Story of Nuns

Copyright © 2024 by Margaret Devereaux

All rights reserved. No part of this book may be reproduced, distributed, or transmitted in any form or by any means, including photocopying, recording, or other electronic or mechanical methods, without the prior written permission of the publisher, except in the case of brief quotations embodied in critical reviews and certain other non-commercial uses permitted by copyright law. For permission requests, the author should be contacted directly.

Dedicated to Daniel and Felicity

Contents

Foreword 10
Chapter 1: 13
Early Beginnings (4th-9th Century) 13
The Birth of Christian Monasticism 13
Women in Early Monasticism 14
Convents in Europe 15
The Spread of Female Monasticism 16
Convents in Early Medieval Society 18
The Influence of the Rule of St. Benedict 19
Chapter 2: 20
The Medieval Era (10th-15th Century) 20
The Expansion of Monastic Orders 20
Daily Life in Medieval Convents 22
Nuns and the Arts 23
The Challenges of Monastic Life 24
Nuns in Society 26
Chapter 3: 28
The Renaissance (15th-17th Century) 28
New Opportunities for Nuns 28
Art and Music in Renaissance Convents 29
The Protestant Reformation 31
The Counter-Reformation 32
The Jesuits and Female Education 34
Chapter 4: 35
Enlightenment to the Modern Era 35
Ideas and New Challenges 35
The French Revolution 37

The 19th Century 38
The Industrial Revolution 39
War, Secularization, and Renewal 40
Chapter 5: 43
Contemporary Nuns (20th-21st Century) 43
Post-Vatican II 43
The Decline in Vocations 44
Nuns and Social Justice 46
Nuns and the Environment 47
Globalization and Interfaith Dialogue 48
The Future of Female Monasticism 49
Chapter 6: 50
Nuns in the Modern World 50
The Global Influence of Nuns 50
Nuns and Healthcare 52
Education and Empowerment 53
The Modern Era 54
Nuns and the Future 56
Chapter 7: 57
Nuns in the 21st Century Convent 57
The Daily Rhythm 57
Work as Worship 58
Community Life 60
Rituals of Initiation and Commitment 61
Engaging with the Outside World 62
The Challenges of Modern Monastic Life 63
Chapter 8: 64
Celebrations and Calendar Events 64
The Liturgical Year 64

Major Feast Days and Solemnities 67
Celebrations of Profession and Jubilee 68
Pilgrimages and Retreats 69
The Role of Community in Celebrations 70
Chapter 9: 72
Statistical Overview of Monastic Life 72
Percentage of Women Who Become Nuns ... 72
Nuns Who Remain in Religious Life 73
Celibacy and Abstinence 74
Age and Demographics of Nuns 75
Educational Background and Roles 76
Vocational Trends 77
The Oldest Recorded Nun 77
The Oldest Living Nun 78
Notable Mentions 79
Chapter 10: 80
Nuns in Hollywood: Reverence to Horror ... 80
Nuns in Popular Media 80
Nuns in Horror Films 82
Why Horror Loves Nuns 83
The Impact of These Portrayals 85
Conclusion: 86
The Legacy of Female Monasticism 86
Notable Nuns in History: 89
Notable Living Nuns 92
Bibliography 95

Beyond the Cloister

The Story of Nuns

Foreword

A few years ago, I found myself standing before the towering gates of a secluded monastery nestled in the rolling hills of rural Italy. I had been invited to spend a week with a community of nuns—an opportunity that I approached with both curiosity and a little apprehension. My journey to this remote place was driven by a desire to escape the hustle and bustle of everyday life, to seek quiet reflection, and perhaps, to understand more deeply a way of life that had always intrigued me from afar.

As the gates creaked open, I was greeted by the warm and serene faces of the sisters who called this place home. They led me into their world, one marked by a rhythm of prayer, work, and contemplation, unlike anything I had ever experienced. The simplicity of their daily routine was striking, yet within that simplicity, I discovered a profound depth of purpose and spiritual fulfillment. During my stay, I observed the nuns as they moved through their day—rising before dawn to chant the Liturgy of the Hours, tending to their gardens, preparing meals, and engaging in silent reflection. Their lives were deeply intertwined with centuries-old traditions, yet they also embraced aspects of modernity with a graceful balance that I found both surprising and inspiring. Conversations with the sisters revealed their individual stories, their challenges, and their joys. Some had entered the convent as young women, while others had made the choice later in life. Each one spoke of a calling that had led them to this place, a calling that was at once deeply personal and universally resonant. Their dedication to their faith, their community, and the broader world around them left an indelible mark on me.

As I prepared to leave the monastery, I realized that my time there had ignited a spark—a desire to learn more about these women and the rich history of female monasticism. I delved into the histories of nuns who had lived centuries ago and those who are shaping the future of religious life today. I explored the cultural, social, and spiritual significance of monasticism, and I sought to understand how these women have navigated the challenges of a changing world while remaining steadfast in their commitments.

This book is the culmination of that journey. It is an attempt to share the stories of nuns from the earliest days of Christianity to the present, to shed light on the lives they lead, the rituals they observe, and the impact they have made—often quietly but powerfully—on the world. It is a tribute to the women I met in that Italian monastery and to all the nuns who have dedicated their lives to a path that is both ancient and ever-relevant. I hope that as you turn these pages, you will come to appreciate the profound contributions of these women, their resilience, and their unwavering devotion. Whether you are familiar with monastic life or approaching it for the first time, I invite you to join me on this journey of discovery, as we explore the rich and fascinating world of female monasticism.

— Margaret Devereaux

Chapter 1:

Early Beginnings (4th-9th Century)

The story of nuns in Europe is deeply intertwined with the broader history of Christian monasticism, a movement that emerged during a period of immense transformation in the late Roman Empire. As the Western Roman Empire declined, new forms of religious life began to take root, laying the foundation for the development of female monastic communities across Europe.

The Birth of Christian Monasticism

Monasticism in Christianity began in the deserts of Egypt and the Near East in the 3rd and 4th centuries. The early Christian hermits, known as "desert fathers and mothers," sought to live in isolation, dedicating their lives to prayer, fasting, and spiritual contemplation. This movement was partly a response to the increasing institutionalization of Christianity within the Roman Empire and a desire to return to what these early ascetics saw as the purity of the apostolic age.

The life of St. Anthony of Egypt (c. 251-356), one of the most famous of the desert fathers, was instrumental in shaping the monastic ideal. His life, as chronicled by St. Athanasius in The Life of Anthony, became a model for those seeking to live a life devoted entirely to God. Anthony's example inspired others to adopt a similar lifestyle, leading to the formation of small communities of ascetics who supported one another in their spiritual endeavours.

These early monastic communities were initially informal and loosely organized, but as their numbers grew, there was a need for more structured forms of communal living. The establishment of formal rules or guidelines became essential to maintain order and harmony within these groups. This led to the development of monastic "rules," which provided a framework for daily life, balancing the demands of prayer, work, and communal living.

Women in Early Monasticism

While the early monastic movement was initially dominated by men, women were also drawn to this ascetic way of life. These early female ascetics, or "desert mothers," lived in solitude or in small, informal groups, often in the same regions as their male counterparts. They sought to emulate the lives of the apostles and early Christian martyrs, believing that through renunciation of worldly pleasures, they could attain spiritual purity and closeness to God.

One of the earliest known female monastics in the Christian tradition was St. Syncletica of Alexandria (c. 270-350), who lived as a hermit in the Egyptian desert. Her teachings and sayings were collected in the *Apophthegmata Patrum* (Sayings of the Desert Fathers), where she is portrayed as a wise and revered spiritual leader. Syncletica's life and teachings had a profound influence on subsequent generations of women who sought to live a life dedicated to God. The emergence of female monasticism in Europe can be traced to the spread of Christianity from the Mediterranean world into the western provinces of the Roman Empire. As Christianity gained a foothold in regions such as Italy, Gaul (modern-day France), and the British Isles, the monastic ideal was embraced by both men and women.

Convents in Europe

The formal establishment of convents in Europe began in the 5th and 6th centuries, coinciding with the spread of Christianity throughout the continent. These early convents were often founded by royal or noble women who sought to create spaces where they and others could live a life devoted to prayer and religious observance.

One of the most notable early figures in European female monasticism was St. Scholastica (c. 480-543), the twin sister of St. Benedict of Nursia. Scholastica is traditionally credited with founding a convent near Monte Cassino in Italy, where her brother established the first Benedictine monastery. The convent followed the *Rule of St. Benedict*, a set of guidelines for monastic life that Benedict had written for his monks. This rule emphasized stability, community, and a balance between prayer, work, and study. The *Rule of St. Benedict* became the foundation for monastic life in Western Europe, influencing both male and female monastic communities. It provided a comprehensive guide for daily life in the monastery, including instructions on prayer, manual labour, reading, and communal meals. The *Rule* emphasized humility, obedience, and the renunciation of personal will, values that were central to the monastic ideal. St. Scholastica's convent was one of the earliest examples of a community of women living under the Benedictine Rule. Although little is known about the specifics of her life, Scholastica's legacy is significant. Her convent became a model for other communities of women who sought to live a life of religious devotion, and she is venerated as a saint in the Catholic Church.

The Spread of Female Monasticism

By the 6th and 7th centuries, the monastic movement had spread across Western Europe, and convents were established in various regions. These convents were often founded by queens, princesses, or noblewomen who had renounced their worldly status to devote themselves to a religious life.

In Ireland, St. Brigid of Kildare (c. 451-525) is one of the most significant figures in the history of female monasticism. Brigid is traditionally credited with founding Kildare Abbey, a monastic community that included both monks and nuns. According to legend, Brigid's community was established on the site of a pagan shrine to the goddess Brigid, and she transformed it into a Christian centre of learning and spirituality. Kildare Abbey became one of the most important religious sites in Ireland, attracting scholars, pilgrims, and students from across Europe. Brigid's leadership and organizational skills were widely admired, and she became known as one of the "three patron saints" of Ireland, alongside St. Patrick and St. Columba. Her abbey set a precedent for other double monasteries, where men and women lived and worked together under the same rule, although in separate quarters.

On the continent, the Merovingian queen Radegund (c. 520-587) founded the Abbey of the Holy Cross at Poitiers in the 6th century. Radegund was originally a Thuringian princess who was captured and married to the Frankish king Clotaire I. After enduring a difficult and unhappy marriage, she fled the royal court and sought refuge in the church. With the support of the bishop of Poitiers, Radegund established her abbey, which became a refuge for women who wished to dedicate their lives to God.

The Abbey of the Holy Cross was unique in that it housed a relic of the True Cross, a fragment of the cross on which Jesus was crucified. This relic made the abbey a major pilgrimage site and increased its prestige. Radegund's community followed a strict ascetic rule, emphasizing prayer, fasting, and manual labour. Her abbey played a crucial role in the development of female monasticism in France and became a model for other convents in the region.

Convents in Early Medieval Society

Convents in early medieval Europe were not merely places of religious seclusion; they were also centres of learning, culture, and social service. Nuns were often well-educated, particularly in reading and writing Latin, the language of the church. Many convents had scriptoria, where nuns copied and preserved religious texts, as well as classical works of literature and philosophy. This work was crucial in preserving knowledge during a time when much of Europe was experiencing political instability and decline.

In addition to their intellectual contributions, nuns played a vital role in the care of the poor and sick. Many convents operated hospices and infirmaries, providing medical care and shelter to those in need. The charitable activities of nuns were seen as a natural extension of their religious devotion, embodying the Christian ideals of compassion and service. Moreover, convents offered women a rare opportunity for leadership and independence in a society that otherwise limited their roles. The abbess, or leader of the convent, held significant authority within the community, overseeing the spiritual and practical aspects of convent life. Some abbesses, such as St. Hilda of Whitby (c. 614-680) in England, became influential figures beyond their convents, advising kings and bishops on matters of religion and governance.

The Influence of the Rule of St. Benedict

The *Rule of St. Benedict* was instrumental in shaping the daily life and spiritual practices of nuns in early medieval Europe. Written in the early 6th century, the *Rule* provided a detailed guide for monastic living, covering all aspects of life in the monastery, from the organization of communal prayer (the Divine Office) to the distribution of work and the management of resources.

One of the key principles of the *Rule* was the concept of "ora et labora" (prayer and work). Monastic life was to be a balance between spiritual activities, such as prayer and reading, and manual labour, which was seen as a way to cultivate humility and avoid idleness. The *Rule* also emphasized the importance of community life, with monks and nuns living together in harmony under the guidance of their abbot or abbess. The *Rule* was both flexible and adaptable, allowing it to be applied to different monastic communities across Europe. Its emphasis on moderation, humility, and obedience made it a practical and enduring framework for monastic life. By the 9th century, the *Rule of St. Benedict* had become the standard for monastic communities throughout Western Europe, influencing the development of both male and female monasticism.

Chapter 2:

The Medieval Era (10th-15th Century)

As Europe transitioned from the early medieval period into the High and Late Middle Ages, the role and influence of monastic life, particularly for women, expanded significantly. This era saw the flourishing of female monasticism, marked by the establishment of new religious orders, the founding of numerous convents, and the increasing involvement of nuns in various aspects of medieval society. The period from the 10th to the 15th century was characterized by both spiritual renewal and social upheaval, shaping the lives of nuns and the communities they served.

The Expansion of Monastic Orders

The 10th and 11th centuries witnessed a revival of monasticism across Europe, often referred to as the "Monastic Reform Movement." This movement sought to renew religious fervour and adherence to the *Rule of St. Benedict*, which had sometimes been neglected in previous centuries. One of the most significant centres of this reform was the Abbey of Cluny in Burgundy, founded in 910 by William I, Duke of Aquitaine. The Cluniac Reforms emphasized strict observance of the *Rule of St. Benedict*, elaborate liturgical practices, and the centralization of monastic authority. While Cluny itself was a male monastery, the Cluniac influence extended to female monasticism. Convents associated with Cluny adopted similar reforms, focusing on the spiritual and liturgical life of the nuns. These reforms led to the establishment of new convents and the revitalization of existing ones, spreading across France, Germany, and beyond.

In addition to the Cluniac Reforms, other monastic orders emerged during this period, offering women different expressions of religious life. The Cistercians, founded in 1098 by St. Robert of Molesme, placed a renewed emphasis on manual labour, simplicity, and a return to the original spirit of the *Rule of St. Benedict*. The first Cistercian convent, the Abbey of Tart, was founded in 1125 near Dijon, France. This marked the beginning of a Cistercian network of female convents across Europe, where nuns lived in austere environments, dedicating themselves to prayer and work in isolation from the outside world.

Another important development was the establishment of the mendicant orders in the 13th century, particularly the Franciscans and Dominicans. Unlike the earlier monastic orders, which were largely cloistered, the mendicant orders focused on preaching, teaching, and serving the poor. Although the primary focus of these orders was on male friars, they also included female branches. St. Clare of Assisi, a close follower of St. Francis, founded the Poor Clares in 1212, a contemplative order that adhered to a life of poverty and prayer. The Poor Clares spread rapidly across Europe, offering women a new model of religious life that combined asceticism with active engagement in their communities.

Daily Life in Medieval Convents

The daily life of a nun in the medieval period was governed by a strict routine cantered on prayer, work, and communal living. The day typically began in the early hours of the morning with the first of eight canonical hours of prayer, known as Matins, followed by Lauds at dawn. These prayers were part of the Divine Office, a series of liturgical prayers recited at regular intervals throughout the day, which included Prime, Terce, Sext, None, Vespers, and Compline. In addition to the Divine Office, nuns attended Mass, engaged in private prayer and meditation, and participated in communal reading of religious texts. The rest of the day was divided between manual labour, such as gardening, weaving, or other tasks necessary for the upkeep of the convent, and intellectual pursuits. Many convents had scriptoria, where nuns copied and illuminated manuscripts, contributing to the preservation and dissemination of religious and classical texts.

Education played a central role in the life of medieval nuns. Convents were often centres of learning, where nuns were trained in reading, writing, and Latin, the language of the church and scholarship. Some convents, especially those affiliated with the Cluniac and Cistercian movements, became renowned for their intellectual activities. The education of nuns was not limited to religious instruction; they were also taught subjects such as music, mathematics, and medicine, skills they used to serve their communities.

Medieval convents also served as places of refuge and education for young women from noble families. These girls, often referred to as "oblates," were placed in convents by their families either as a form of religious vocation or as a way to receive an education. While some oblates eventually took vows and became nuns, others returned to secular life, bringing with them the knowledge and skills they had acquired in the convent.

Nuns and the Arts

The medieval period was a time of rich artistic and cultural production, and nuns played a significant role in this creative flourishing. Convents were centres of artistic activity, particularly in the fields of manuscript illumination, embroidery, and music.

Manuscript illumination, the art of decorating handwritten books with intricate designs, flourished in many medieval convents. Nuns created beautifully decorated Psalters, Books of Hours, and other religious texts, which were often commissioned by wealthy patrons. These illuminated manuscripts not only served as objects of devotion but also as demonstrations of the artistic skill and devotion of the nuns who created them. Embroidery was another important artistic endeavor in medieval convents. Nuns produced elaborate embroidered vestments, altar cloths, and banners for use in religious ceremonies. The art of embroidery required both technical skill and artistic creativity, and it was often seen as a form of meditation, with the repetitive motions of stitching helping to focus the mind on prayer.

Music also played a central role in the life of medieval nuns. The Divine Office was sung in chant, and many convents had choirs that performed complex polyphonic music. Some nuns, such as the German abbess and composer Hildegard of Bingen (1098-1179), made significant contributions to the development of medieval music. Hildegard's compositions, which include liturgical songs and hymns, are among the earliest known works of music composed by a woman. Her music reflects both her deep spirituality and her innovative approach to the liturgical traditions of her time.

The Challenges of Monastic Life

Despite the spiritual rewards and creative opportunities that convent life offered, medieval nuns also faced significant challenges. The demands of religious observance, combined with the often harsh living conditions in some convents, required a high degree of physical and mental endurance. Fasting, long hours of prayer, and the austere lifestyle prescribed by the *Rule* could take a toll on the health of the nuns, particularly in communities where food and medical care were scarce.

In addition to these physical challenges, nuns also had to navigate complex social and political dynamics within their convents and the wider society. The leadership of a convent, typically held by the abbess, was a position of significant responsibility and authority. However, the abbess also had to manage relationships with the church hierarchy, local lords, and the families of the nuns, all of whom could exert pressure on the convent's operations. Conflicts sometimes arose within convents over issues such as the interpretation of the *Rule*, the distribution of resources, or the admission of new members. These disputes could lead to divisions within the community or even the dissolution of a convent. In some cases, external pressures, such as war, famine, or political upheaval, forced convents to relocate or close entirely.

The broader societal attitudes toward women and religion also posed challenges for medieval nuns. While the church provided a framework for female religious life, it also imposed strict limitations on the roles that women could play within the church and society. Nuns were expected to live in cloistered seclusion, with limited contact with the outside world. This restriction, while intended to protect the spiritual purity of the nuns, also limited their ability to engage with the broader community.

Despite these challenges, many nuns found ways to exert influence both within and beyond their convents. Some abbesses, such as Heloise d'Argenteuil, corresponded with prominent intellectuals and theologians, contributing to the intellectual and religious debates of their time. Others, like Hildegard of Bingen, used their spiritual authority and creative talents to gain recognition as leaders in the church.

Nuns in Society

Throughout the medieval period, nuns played a vital role in the social fabric of European society. Convents were not only centres of spiritual life but also of education, healthcare, and charity. Nuns were often the first line of support for the poor, sick, and vulnerable, providing services that were essential to the wellbeing of their communities.

Education was one of the most significant contributions of medieval convents. In a time when educational opportunities for women were limited, convents provided a space where girls could receive instruction in reading, writing, and other subjects. Some convents, particularly those associated with the Cluniac and Cistercian movements, became renowned centres of learning, attracting students and scholars from across Europe. Nuns were also deeply involved in healthcare, often running infirmaries and hospices within their convents. They provided medical care to both the residents of the convent and the surrounding community, using knowledge passed down through generations of religious women. This included not only the treatment of physical ailments but also the spiritual care of the dying, a role that was seen as a sacred duty.

The influence of nuns extended beyond the walls of the convent. Some abbesses wielded considerable power in the secular world, managing large estates and engaging in diplomacy with local rulers. In some regions, abbesses were granted the status of feudal lords, with authority over land and subjects. This gave them a unique position of power and influence, allowing them to advocate for the interests of their convents and the church.

Chapter 3:

The Renaissance (15th-17th Century)

As Europe entered the Renaissance and Reformation periods, profound changes swept through its political, intellectual, and religious landscapes. The role of female monasticism was significantly affected by these transformations, with nuns facing both new opportunities and considerable challenges. The rise of humanism during the Renaissance opened up new educational opportunities for some women, while the Protestant Reformation and Catholic Counter-Reformation brought both upheaval and reform to religious life. This chapter explores how nuns navigated these turbulent times, contributing to both religious renewal and social change.

New Opportunities for Nuns

The Renaissance, which began in Italy in the 14th century and spread throughout Europe over the following centuries, was characterized by a revival of interest in classical learning and humanist thought. Although the Renaissance is often associated with secular intellectual and artistic achievements, its influence extended into religious life, including the lives of nuns. One of the key features of the Renaissance was its emphasis on education and intellectual development, particularly the study of classical texts from ancient Greece and Rome. While women were largely excluded from formal education, some convents became centres of learning where nuns engaged with Renaissance humanism. In these convents, nuns studied Latin, Greek, and even Hebrew, gaining access to the same classical texts that were being rediscovered by their male counterparts.

A notable example of this intellectual engagement can be seen in the life of Isotta Nogarola (1418-1466), an Italian scholar and writer who, though not a nun, corresponded with leading humanists of her time and influenced the intellectual culture of Italian convents. Her work helped shape the thinking of other learned women within religious communities, demonstrating the potential for intellectual exchange between female monastic communities and the wider scholarly world. In some parts of Europe, convents served as places where women could continue their education and pursue intellectual pursuits in relative independence. For noblewomen, entering a convent could offer an alternative to marriage, allowing them to lead lives of prayer, study, and writing. Nuns such as Laura Cereta (1469-1499), another Italian humanist, produced works that engaged with contemporary debates on women's education and the role of women in society, demonstrating that convents could provide a space for scholarly activity during this period.

Art and Music in Renaissance Convents

The Renaissance's focus on art and culture also permeated convent life. Convents were often important patrons of the arts, commissioning religious paintings, sculptures, and altarpieces for their chapels and churches. Artists such as Fra Angelico, a Dominican friar, and other Renaissance painters were commissioned by convents to produce works that would inspire spiritual devotion.

Nuns themselves were often accomplished artists and musicians. In the realm of music, the Renaissance saw the development of polyphony, a style of music in which multiple independent melodies are sung simultaneously. Convents became important centres for the composition and performance of polyphonic music, with nuns playing a vital role in its development. One of the most notable composers of sacred music during the Renaissance was the Italian nun and composer Raffaella Aleotti (c. 1570-1646), who composed intricate polyphonic works for her convent in Ferrara. Her music represents some of the earliest known compositions by a woman in the Renaissance.

Convents also produced visual art, particularly illuminated manuscripts, textiles, and tapestries. The production of religious art within convents was often seen as a form of worship, with the artistic process serving as a meditative and devotional act. Embroidery, in particular, was a skill practiced by many nuns, and the elaborately embroidered vestments and altar cloths they produced were used in religious ceremonies and processions.

The Protestant Reformation

The 16th century brought dramatic religious upheaval with the onset of the Protestant Reformation, a movement that challenged the authority and practices of the Catholic Church. Initiated by figures like Martin Luther in 1517, the Reformation rejected many aspects of Catholic doctrine, including the monastic life itself. Protestant reformers criticized what they saw as the corruption and excesses of monasteries and convents, advocating for a return to a simpler form of Christianity focused on scripture and individual faith.

One of the central tenets of Protestant theology was the rejection of the monastic vows of celibacy, poverty, and obedience. Reformers argued that such vows were unnecessary and that religious life should be accessible to all believers, not confined to cloistered communities. As a result, many convents were closed or repurposed in Protestant regions, particularly in Germany, Switzerland, and Scandinavia.

In the early years of the Reformation, some nuns voluntarily left their convents to join the Protestant movement, rejecting their vows and seeking new lives outside the cloister. One of the most famous examples is Katharina von Bora (1499-1552), a former Cistercian nun who became the wife of Martin Luther. After escaping her convent, Katharina became an important figure in the Reformation, managing the Luther household and supporting her husband's theological work.

However, not all nuns were eager to leave their convents. Many resisted the closure of their communities, and in some cases, they faced persecution or displacement. The dissolution of convents often had severe consequences for the women who had dedicated their lives to religious service, forcing them into a society that provided few alternatives for women outside of marriage or the family.

The Counter-Reformation

In response to the Protestant Reformation, the Catholic Church launched the Counter-Reformation, a movement aimed at reforming the church and reaffirming Catholic doctrine. One of the central goals of the Counter-Reformation was to address the criticisms leveled at monastic life by Protestant reformers and to renew the spiritual vitality of convents and monasteries.

The Council of Trent (1545-1563), a key event in the Counter-Reformation, issued decrees aimed at reforming the Catholic Church's institutions, including convents. One of the council's main concerns was the enforcement of strict enclosure for nuns, a practice that required nuns to remain isolated from the outside world in order to focus on prayer and spiritual contemplation. While some convents had previously allowed nuns to engage in charitable activities outside the cloister, the Council of Trent insisted on strict enclosure, reinforcing the idea that nuns' primary role was to live a life of seclusion and prayer. The council's emphasis on enclosure had a significant impact on the daily lives of nuns, limiting their ability to engage with the broader community and restricting their involvement in activities such as education and charity. However, this renewed focus on spiritual discipline also provided an opportunity for reform and revitalization within convents. Many convents embraced the changes introduced by the Council of Trent, adopting stricter rules and devoting themselves to the spiritual renewal of their communities.

One of the most important figures of the Counter-Reformation was St. Teresa of Ávila (1515-1582), a Spanish Carmelite nun and mystic who played a leading role in the reform of the Carmelite order. Teresa founded several convents in Spain that adhered to a stricter form of the Carmelite rule, emphasizing poverty, prayer, and contemplation. Her reforms, known as the Discalced Carmelite movement, spread across Europe, inspiring a wave of spiritual renewal within the Catholic Church. Teresa's influence extended beyond the walls of the convent. Her writings, including *The Interior Castle* and *The Way of Perfection*, became widely read and admired for their spiritual insights and practical guidance on the contemplative life. Teresa's legacy as a reformer and mystic earned her canonization in 1622, and she remains one of the most important female figures in the history of the Catholic Church.

The Jesuits and Female Education

During the Counter-Reformation, new religious orders dedicated to education and missionary work were established, with the Jesuits being one of the most influential. While the Jesuits themselves were an all-male order, their emphasis on education inspired the formation of new female religious communities that focused on teaching and catechism. One such community was the Ursuline order, founded in 1535 by St. Angela Merici in Brescia, Italy. The Ursulines were one of the first female religious orders to focus specifically on the education of girls. Unlike many other convents, which were enclosed and focused primarily on contemplative life, the Ursulines were active in their communities, establishing schools for girls and providing religious instruction to young women.

The spread of the Ursulines across Europe and beyond marked a significant development in the role of nuns in education. By the late 16th and early 17th centuries, Ursuline convents had been established in France, Germany, the Netherlands, and the New World. The Ursulines played a key role in the Catholic Church's efforts to counter the influence of Protestantism, particularly by educating girls in Catholic doctrine and values.

Chapter 4:

Enlightenment to the Modern Era

The journey of female monasticism from the 18th to the 20th century is a story of resilience and adaptation. As Europe experienced profound shifts in thought, society, and politics, nuns faced the challenge of staying true to their spiritual commitments while responding to a rapidly changing world. This chapter explores how convents navigated the intellectual challenges of the Enlightenment, the social upheavals of the Industrial Revolution, and the trials of two world wars, all while continuing to play vital roles in their communities.

Ideas and New Challenges

The Enlightenment was a period in the 18th century when thinkers across Europe began to question traditional authority and emphasize reason, science, and individual rights. This movement had a significant impact on religion, as many Enlightenment thinkers were critical of the Catholic Church and its practices. Monastic life, with its vows of poverty, chastity, and obedience, was often seen as outdated and unnecessary in an age that valued progress and practical contributions to society.

Voltaire, one of the most famous Enlightenment philosophers, criticized monasteries and convents as places of idleness and superstition. He and others argued that the resources and energy spent on maintaining religious communities could be better used to benefit society in more tangible ways. These critiques led to increased pressure on religious communities to justify their existence and demonstrate their value to the broader society. In response to these challenges, many convents sought to expand their roles beyond the cloister. They became more involved in education, healthcare, and charity work, areas that were becoming increasingly important in the changing social landscape of Europe. Convents established schools, particularly for girls, and provided essential medical care in hospitals they founded and managed. By doing so, they aligned themselves with some Enlightenment ideals, such as the promotion of knowledge and the improvement of human welfare, while maintaining their religious commitments.

However, the spread of Enlightenment ideas also led to the suppression of many religious communities, especially in regions where secular authorities gained power. In Austria, for example, Emperor Joseph II, influenced by Enlightenment thinking, implemented reforms known as Josephinism in the late 18th century. These reforms sought to reduce the influence of the Catholic Church and included the closure of many monasteries and convents that were deemed "unproductive." The state seized their properties, and many nuns were forced to leave their communities.

The French Revolution

The French Revolution, which began in 1789, was one of the most dramatic periods of change in European history. It brought about the end of the monarchy, the rise of a secular republic, and a radical restructuring of French society. The revolutionaries saw the Catholic Church as a symbol of the old order, and they sought to dismantle its power and influence. One of the most significant actions taken by the revolutionary government was the passing of the Civil Constitution of the Clergy in 1790. This law brought the Catholic Church in France under state control and required all clergy, including nuns, to swear allegiance to the state rather than the pope. Many nuns refused to take this oath, leading to the closure of their convents and the seizure of their properties. Those who resisted were often forced to leave their communities and return to secular life, which had been radically transformed by the revolution.

The Reign of Terror (1793-1794) saw even harsher measures against those who were perceived as enemies of the revolution. Religious figures who continued to practice their faith openly were often arrested and executed. One of the most tragic examples of this persecution was the execution of the 16 Carmelite Martyrs of Compiègne in 1794. These nuns were guillotined in Paris for refusing to disband their convent and renounce their faith. Their martyrdom became a powerful symbol of religious resistance in the face of revolutionary violence.

After the revolution, the Concordat of 1801, an agreement between Napoleon Bonaparte and Pope Pius VII, sought to restore some degree of religious stability in France. However, the damage had already been done. Many convents remained closed, and those that reopened often operated under strict state supervision. The French Revolution left a lasting impact on female monasticism, forcing nuns to navigate a new political and social landscape that was often hostile to their way of life.

The 19th Century

Despite the challenges of the Enlightenment and the French Revolution, the 19th century brought a period of renewal for female monasticism. Across Europe, there was a resurgence of religious fervour, often referred to as the "Catholic Revival." This movement was characterized by a renewed emphasis on traditional Catholic practices, including the veneration of saints and the establishment of new religious orders.

Many of these new orders focused on active engagement with society, particularly in education, healthcare, and social services. The Sisters of Charity, founded in the 17th century by St. Vincent de Paul, became a model for these new communities. Unlike traditional enclosed orders, the Sisters of Charity were not bound by strict cloistered life, allowing them to work directly with the people they served. Their focus on caring for the poor, the sick, and the marginalized resonated with the growing social consciousness of the time. Other orders, such as the Daughters of Charity and the Sisters of Mercy, spread rapidly across Europe and beyond. They established schools for girls, ran hospitals, and provided shelter for orphans and the destitute. These orders played a crucial role in addressing the social problems that arose during the Industrial Revolution, a period marked by rapid urbanization, poverty, and poor working conditions.

The 19th century also saw a significant expansion of missionary work by female religious orders. Nuns from Europe travelled to distant parts of the world, including Africa, Asia, and the Americas, where they established schools, hospitals, and orphanages. These missionary efforts were often closely linked to European colonial expansion, and while they brought education and healthcare to many, they were also part of the broader imposition of European cultural values on colonized peoples.

The Industrial Revolution

The Industrial Revolution, which began in the late 18th century and continued into the 19th century, transformed Europe's social and economic landscape. The rapid growth of cities and the shift from rural, agrarian economies to urban, industrial ones created new challenges, including widespread poverty, disease, and poor living conditions. Nuns were among the first to respond to these pressing social needs.

Convents in industrial cities established schools to educate the children of working-class families, who were often neglected in the rush to industrialize. These schools provided basic education, including reading, writing, and arithmetic, as well as moral and religious instruction. For many children, these convent-run schools were the only opportunity for education they had.

In addition to education, nuns played a vital role in healthcare during this period. They founded hospitals and clinics in some of the most impoverished areas, where they provided medical care to the sick and injured. Nuns also set up orphanages to care for children who had lost their parents, often due to the harsh conditions of industrial life. Their work was driven by a deep sense of religious duty and the belief that they were called to serve the most vulnerable members of society. This period also saw the rise of Catholic social teaching, which emphasized the dignity of work, the rights of workers, and the importance of social justice. Nuns were at the forefront of putting these teachings into practice, often working in the most challenging and impoverished environments. Their efforts helped to bridge the gap between the church and the rapidly industrializing society, demonstrating that religious life could adapt to and address the pressing issues of the modern world.

War, Secularization, and Renewal

The 20th century was marked by two world wars, political upheaval, and significant changes in European society.

These events had a profound impact on female monasticism, as nuns were called upon to respond to the challenges of war, totalitarian regimes, and the continuing secularization of society. During both World War I and World War II, nuns played a crucial role in providing medical care, shelter, and support to soldiers and civilians alike. Convents were often converted into makeshift hospitals and shelters, and nuns worked tirelessly to care for the wounded and displaced. In occupied countries, some nuns were involved in resistance efforts, hiding refugees, including Jews, from Nazi persecution. Their bravery and dedication during these conflicts earned them widespread respect and admiration.

However, the post-war period also brought new challenges, particularly with the rise of secularization and the decline of religious vocations. The secularization of European society, driven by factors such as the decline of traditional religious authority, the rise of scientific and technological advancements, and the increasing emphasis on individualism, led to a decrease in the number of women entering convents. Many convents closed due to a lack of new members, and those that remained open often faced financial difficulties.

In response to these challenges, the Catholic Church sought to renew and adapt monastic life to the modern world. The Second Vatican Council (1962-1965), one of the most significant events in the history of the Catholic Church, introduced reforms aimed at modernizing the church and making it more relevant to contemporary society. For female monasticism, this meant a revaluation of traditional practices, including the vow of enclosure, the role of nuns in society, and the relationship between religious life and the broader community.

Some convents embraced the changes introduced by Vatican II, becoming more involved in social justice work, education, and community outreach. Nuns began to engage more actively with the world outside the cloister, taking on new roles that allowed them to continue their religious mission while also addressing the needs of a rapidly changing world.

Chapter 5:

Contemporary Nuns (20th-21st Century)

As the world entered the late 20th and early 21st centuries, the role of nuns and female monasticism continued to evolve. Modernization, technological advancements, and globalization have brought new challenges and opportunities for religious life. This chapter explores how nuns have navigated the contemporary era, embracing change while remaining committed to their spiritual vocations. It also examines how the global context has influenced their work and the ways in which they have redefined their roles in a rapidly shifting world.

Post-Vatican II

The Second Vatican Council (1962-1965), commonly known as Vatican II, was a watershed moment in the history of the Catholic Church. The council aimed to address the needs of the modern world and sought to bring the church into greater dialogue with contemporary society. For nuns, the changes introduced by Vatican II were both profound and far-reaching. One of the most significant changes was the revaluation of the vow of enclosure. Traditionally, nuns lived in cloistered communities, separated from the outside world to focus on prayer and contemplation. Vatican II encouraged a re-examination of this practice, suggesting that nuns might engage more directly with society while still maintaining their spiritual focus. This shift led many nuns to become more involved in social justice work, education, healthcare, and other forms of community outreach.

The council also emphasized the importance of religious communities adapting to the cultural and social contexts in which they lived. This led to a greater diversity of religious life, with nuns taking on new roles that aligned with the needs of their local communities. For example, in Latin America, nuns became deeply involved in the liberation theology movement, working alongside the poor and marginalized to promote social justice and human rights.

In the United States and Europe, many nuns took on roles as educators, healthcare providers, and social workers, often in underserved communities. These new ministries reflected a broader understanding of religious life as being not only about personal sanctity but also about active engagement with the world. This era of renewal and reassessment allowed nuns to redefine their roles in ways that were both relevant and meaningful in the modern context.

The Decline in Vocations

One of the most significant challenges faced by female monasticism in the contemporary era has been the decline in religious vocations. Beginning in the late 20th century, fewer women chose to enter convents, a trend driven by several factors, including changing social attitudes, greater opportunities for women in secular professions, and the secularization of society.

This decline has led to the closure of many convents, particularly in Europe and North America, where the aging population of nuns has not been replaced by new members. Those convents that have remained open often face financial difficulties and must find new ways to sustain themselves and their missions. In response to these challenges, many religious communities have adapted by forming new types of religious life that are less traditional but still deeply rooted in spiritual practice. Some convents have embraced more flexible forms of community life, where members may live outside the convent but still participate in the community's spiritual and service-oriented activities. These new models reflect a changing understanding of what it means to be a nun in the modern world, allowing for greater engagement with society while maintaining a commitment to religious life.

Additionally, some convents have turned to new forms of income generation, such as offering retreat centres, running educational programs, or producing artisanal goods. These efforts not only help sustain the convents financially but also allow them to share their spiritual practices with a broader audience.

Nuns and Social Justice

One of the most significant developments in contemporary female monasticism has been the increasing involvement of nuns in social justice issues. Inspired by the teachings of Vatican II and the examples of figures like Dorothy Day and Mother Teresa, nuns have become active in addressing some of the most pressing social issues of our time, including poverty, immigration, environmental sustainability, and human rights. In Latin America, the liberation theology movement, which emerged in the 1960s and 1970s, saw nuns taking a leading role in advocating for the poor and oppressed. These nuns worked in solidarity with marginalized communities, challenging unjust social structures and advocating for systemic change. Their work often put them at odds with both political authorities and the church hierarchy, but they remained committed to their mission of social justice.

In the United States, nuns have been at the forefront of movements for civil rights, immigration reform, and environmental protection. Groups like the Leadership Conference of Women Religious (LCWR) have been vocal advocates for justice and peace, often taking stands on controversial issues that have brought them into conflict with more conservative elements of the church. One of the most visible examples of nuns' involvement in social justice is the "Nuns on the Bus" campaign, which began in 2012. Organized by Sister Simone Campbell and her organization

NETWORK, the campaign involved nuns traveling across the United States to advocate for economic justice, healthcare reform, and immigration rights. The "Nuns on the Bus" became a powerful symbol of the role that nuns can play in public life, using their moral authority to speak out on behalf of those who are often voiceless.

Nuns and the Environment

As awareness of environmental issues has grown in recent decades, many nuns have taken up the cause of environmental stewardship as part of their religious mission. Inspired by the concept of "integral ecology," which sees care for the environment as inseparable from care for the poor and vulnerable, nuns have become active in efforts to protect the planet.

In various parts of the world, nuns have led initiatives to promote sustainable agriculture, protect natural resources, and educate communities about environmental issues. For example, the Benedictine Sisters of Erie, Pennsylvania, have transformed their monastery grounds into a model of environmental sustainability, with organic gardens, solar panels, and conservation programs. Their work reflects a broader movement within female monasticism to live in harmony with the environment and to advocate for policies that protect the earth. In some cases, nuns have also engaged in direct action to defend the environment. In the Amazon rainforest, where deforestation and mining threaten both the environment and indigenous communities, nuns have been involved in efforts to protect the land and its people. Their work often involves collaboration with local communities, NGOs, and other religious groups, reflecting a growing recognition of the interconnectedness of all life.

Globalization and Interfaith Dialogue

The contemporary era has also seen nuns engaging more actively in interfaith dialogue and collaboration, reflecting the increasingly interconnected and globalized world in which they live. Nuns have taken part in initiatives that promote understanding and cooperation between different religious traditions, recognizing that many of the world's most pressing problems, such as poverty, conflict, and environmental degradation, require collective action. In countries like India, where religious diversity is the norm, nuns have worked alongside women of other faiths to address common social issues, such as human trafficking, education, and healthcare. These efforts often involve a deep commitment to mutual respect and understanding, as well as a recognition of the shared values that unite different religious traditions.

In the West, nuns have also participated in interfaith dialogue, particularly in response to global challenges like climate change and migration. By building bridges between different religious communities, nuns have contributed to a more inclusive and cooperative approach to addressing the issues that affect all of humanity.

The Future of Female Monasticism

As the 21st century progresses, the future of female monasticism remains a topic of both concern and hope. The decline in vocations continues to challenge traditional forms of religious life, and many convents are grappling with the question of how to sustain their missions in a rapidly changing world. However, the adaptability and resilience that have characterized female monasticism throughout history continue to guide these communities as they navigate the complexities of the modern era.

Some religious communities are exploring new forms of religious life that reflect the realities of the contemporary world. These include lay associate programs, where non-vowed members participate in the spiritual and service-oriented activities of the community, and new forms of communal living that emphasize flexibility and engagement with the broader society. These innovations suggest that while the traditional convent may be changing, the core values of female monasticism—prayer, service, and community—remain as relevant as ever.

Moreover, the global nature of contemporary religious life has opened up new opportunities for collaboration and mutual support among nuns from different parts of the world. As nuns continue to engage with the challenges of poverty, injustice, and environmental degradation, their work increasingly reflects a global perspective, rooted in a deep sense of solidarity with all of humanity.

Chapter 6:

Nuns in the Modern World

As we move further into the 21st century, the role of nuns and female monasticism continues to evolve, adapting to both global trends and local needs. This chapter delves into how nuns are shaping the modern world, from their influence on global issues to their impact on local communities. We will explore the diverse ways in which these women contribute to contemporary society, as well as the challenges they face in an increasingly secular and interconnected world.

The Global Influence of Nuns

Nuns have long been at the forefront of social change, and in the modern world, their influence extends across the globe. Through international networks, advocacy work, and direct action, they continue to champion the causes of justice, peace, and human dignity.

One of the key areas where nuns have made a significant impact is in the fight against human trafficking. This modern form of slavery affects millions of people worldwide, particularly women and children. Nuns from various orders have taken up the cause, working to rescue victims, provide them with support and rehabilitation, and advocate for stronger laws to prevent trafficking. A prominent example of this work is the Talitha Kum network, an international organization of Catholic nuns dedicated to combating human trafficking. Founded in 2009, Talitha Kum operates in over 90 countries, coordinating efforts to raise awareness, provide direct assistance to survivors, and advocate for systemic change. The network is named after a phrase from the Gospel of Mark, meaning "Little girl, I say to you, arise," reflecting the mission to restore dignity and life to those who have been exploited.

In addition to their work on human trafficking, nuns have also played a significant role in advocating for environmental sustainability. The environmental movement has gained momentum in recent decades, with increasing awareness of the threats posed by climate change, deforestation, and pollution. Many religious communities, including nuns, have embraced the call to care for the Earth as part of their spiritual mission.

The Sisters of St. Joseph of Carondelet, for example, have been active in promoting environmental justice, working to reduce their carbon footprint, support sustainable agriculture, and advocate for policies that protect the environment. They have also been involved in efforts to raise awareness about the interconnectedness of social and environmental issues, emphasizing that the fight for environmental justice is also a fight for human dignity and equality.

Nuns and Healthcare

Healthcare has always been a central focus of many religious communities, and in the modern world, nuns continue to provide essential medical services, often in underserved or marginalized communities. Their work in healthcare reflects a deep commitment to compassion and care for the most vulnerable, guided by the belief that every person deserves dignity and respect.

In Africa, where access to healthcare can be limited, nuns have been instrumental in providing medical care to communities affected by poverty, conflict, and disease. For instance, the Medical Missionaries of Mary, an international congregation of Catholic nuns founded in 1937, have been working in some of the most challenging environments across the continent. They provide a range of services, from running hospitals and clinics to offering maternal and child healthcare, HIV/AIDS education, and treatment.

During the Ebola outbreak in West Africa between 2014 and 2016, nuns were on the front lines of the response, providing critical care to those affected by the virus and helping to contain its spread. Their presence in remote and underserved areas, coupled with their commitment to serving those in need, made them invaluable to the international efforts to combat the outbreak. In the United States, nuns have also been at the forefront of healthcare, particularly in areas where access to medical services is limited. Many Catholic hospitals across the country were founded and are still operated by religious orders of nuns. These institutions often serve as safety nets for the poor and uninsured, providing care regardless of a patient's ability to pay. The mission of these hospitals is deeply rooted in the religious commitment to serve all people, especially the most vulnerable.

Education and Empowerment

Education has always been a cornerstone of the work of nuns, and in the modern world, their efforts continue to make a significant impact. Nuns have long recognized the power of education to transform lives, particularly for girls and women who might otherwise be denied opportunities for learning and advancement.

In many parts of the world, nuns operate schools and educational programs that provide not only basic literacy and numeracy skills but also a broader education that empowers students to become active and informed citizens. In India, for example, the Loreto Sisters have been involved in education for over 175 years, running schools that serve both urban and rural communities. Their focus on educating girls, in particular, has had a profound impact, breaking cycles of poverty and opening up new possibilities for future generations. In Africa, the Holy Cross Sisters have established schools that prioritize the education of girls, understanding that educating women is key to the development of entire communities. These schools often serve as more than just educational institutions; they are also centres of community life, providing a safe space for girls to learn and grow in environments where they might otherwise face significant barriers.

In the United States and Europe, nuns have been pioneers in higher education, founding and operating colleges and universities that have educated generations of women and men. Institutions like Trinity Washington University, founded by the Sisters of Notre Dame de Namur, and Mount St. Mary's University, founded by the Sisters of Charity, have been leaders in providing quality education rooted in Catholic values. These universities continue to be centres of learning and social engagement, preparing students to be ethical leaders in a complex world.

Beyond formal education, many nuns are involved in programs that empower women through vocational training, leadership development, and advocacy. These programs are often designed to help women gain the skills and confidence they need to take control of their lives and contribute to their communities. For example, the Presentation Sisters in Pakistan run programs that teach women how to read and write, as well as how to develop practical skills such as sewing and embroidery, which can provide a source of income.

The Modern Era

Despite their many contributions, nuns today face significant challenges. The decline in religious vocations, particularly in Europe and North America, has led to the closure of many convents and schools. Aging populations within religious communities, financial pressures, and the secularization of society have also created difficulties for many orders.

However, these challenges have also led to new opportunities for innovation and adaptation. Some religious communities have embraced more flexible models of religious life, allowing members to live outside the convent while still participating in the community's spiritual and service-oriented activities. This flexibility has made religious life more accessible to women who feel called to serve but may not be able to commit to traditional forms of monastic life. In addition, the global nature of contemporary religious life has opened up new possibilities for collaboration and mutual support among nuns from different parts of the world. International networks, such as the International Union of Superiors General (UISG), have facilitated greater communication and cooperation among nuns, allowing them to share resources, ideas, and strategies for addressing common challenges.

Technology has also played a role in modernizing religious life. Many nuns now use social media, websites, and other digital tools to reach broader audiences, share their work, and engage in dialogue with people around the world. These platforms have allowed nuns to connect with younger generations, promote their causes, and demonstrate the relevance of their work in the modern world.

Nuns and the Future

As we look to the future, the role of nuns in the modern world is likely to continue evolving. While traditional forms of religious life may be declining, the values of service, compassion, and community that have always been at the heart of female monasticism remain as relevant as ever.

One of the most promising trends is the increasing involvement of laypeople in the work traditionally done by nuns. Many religious communities have established lay associate programs, where non-vowed members participate in the spiritual and service activities of the community. These programs allow laypeople to engage in meaningful service while maintaining their commitments to family and career. Moreover, the global challenges of our time — such as climate change, migration, and social inequality — will likely continue to draw nuns into new forms of activism and service. As they have done throughout history, nuns will adapt to these challenges, finding innovative ways to live out their calling in a rapidly changing world.

Chapter 7:

Nuns in the 21st Century Convent

The life of a nun in the 21st century, while deeply rooted in centuries-old traditions, also reflects the adaptations and changes that have come with modernity. Nuns today continue to live lives marked by prayer, work, and community, but they do so in a world that has transformed significantly since the early days of monasticism. This chapter explores the daily life and rituals of nuns in contemporary convents, offering a glimpse into the rhythms of their spiritual and communal lives, as well as the ways they balance tradition with the realities of the modern world.

The Daily Rhythm

At the heart of convent life is prayer, which forms the foundation of a nun's daily routine. The structure of the day is typically shaped by the Liturgy of the Hours, a series of prayers recited at specific times throughout the day, from early morning until night. This practice, also known as the Divine Office, is one of the oldest traditions in Christian monasticism, dating back to the early centuries of the church.

In most convents, the day begins with Morning Prayer, often called Lauds, which is typically held at dawn. This prayer is a time to give thanks for the new day and to seek God's guidance and presence throughout the hours ahead. Following Lauds, many nuns participate in the celebration of the Eucharist (Mass), which is the central act of worship in the Catholic tradition. The Eucharist is seen as a vital spiritual nourishment, uniting the community in communion with Christ and with one another. Throughout the day, nuns return to prayer at regular intervals, marking the hours with specific prayers such as Terce (mid-morning), Sext (midday), and None (mid-afternoon). These prayers are usually shorter than Lauds or Vespers (Evening Prayer) and are often recited or chanted in community. The day typically ends with Compline, a prayer that offers thanks for the day that has passed and seeks God's protection through the night.

While the Liturgy of the Hours provides a structured rhythm to the day, many nuns also spend time in personal prayer and meditation. This private time allows for deeper contemplation, reflection on the Scriptures, and a more intimate connection with God. For some, this might involve silent prayer in a chapel or a private cell; for others, it could be a meditative walk in a convent garden.

Work as Worship

In the 21st century, work remains an integral part of monastic life, continuing the Benedictine tradition of "ora et labora" (prayer and work). The concept of work as a form of worship is central to monastic spirituality, with the understanding that all labour, whether physical or intellectual, is a way to glorify God and serve the community.

The types of work that nuns engage in can vary widely depending on the focus of their convent and the needs of the community. Some nuns work in the convent's gardens or kitchens, growing food and preparing meals for the community. Others may be involved in making vestments, altar cloths, or other items used in worship. In some convents, nuns engage in artistic endeavours, such as creating religious icons, writing, or composing music, all seen as expressions of devotion. Many nuns also work outside the convent, particularly those involved in education, healthcare, or social services. Teaching in schools, nursing in hospitals, or providing counselling and support to those in need are all considered extensions of their religious vocation. These activities allow nuns to live out their commitment to service while remaining connected to the world beyond the convent walls.

In some communities, nuns are also involved in various forms of income-generating activities, such as running retreat centres, producing artisanal goods, or managing guesthouses. These endeavours help sustain the convent financially and provide opportunities for outreach and engagement with the broader community.

Community Life

Community life is one of the defining characteristics of monastic life. Nuns live together in a convent or monastery, sharing daily routines, meals, and spiritual practices. This communal living is intended to foster a deep sense of sisterhood and mutual support, where each member contributes to the well-being of the community.

Meals are typically eaten together in a communal dining room, often in silence or accompanied by the reading of spiritual texts. The sharing of meals is an important part of building community, providing a space for reflection, gratitude, and the reinforcement of communal bonds. In many convents, the food is simple, reflecting the vow of poverty and the monastic commitment to a life of simplicity and moderation. Living in community also involves the practice of mutual obedience and respect. Nuns are expected to follow the guidance of their superior, often called an abbess or prioress, who is elected by the community and serves as its spiritual and administrative leader. The vow of obedience is not seen as a loss of personal freedom but as a means of achieving greater spiritual unity and harmony within the community.

Conflict is inevitable in any community, and convents are no exception. However, nuns are encouraged to address disagreements through dialogue, prayer, and a spirit of reconciliation. The goal is always to maintain peace and unity within the community, recognizing that each member plays a vital role in the spiritual and communal life of the convent.

Rituals of Initiation and Commitment

Becoming a nun is a process that involves deep reflection, discernment, and a series of formal steps. The journey begins with a period of candidacy or postulancy, where a woman lives in the convent and participates in its life but has not yet taken formal vows. This period allows her to discern whether she feels called to the monastic life.

If she decides to continue, the next step is the novitiate, a more formal period of training and spiritual formation that typically lasts one to two years. During this time, the novice learns about the history, rules, and spiritual practices of the community. She also deepens her prayer life and begins to fully integrate into the life of the convent. At the end of the novitiate, the novice may take temporary vows, committing herself to the monastic life for a period of time, often three to five years. These vows typically include poverty, chastity, and obedience, which are the traditional vows of religious life in the Catholic Church. Temporary vows are seen as a time of deeper commitment and continued discernment, allowing the woman to live fully as a nun while still having the option to leave if she feels that the life is not her calling.

After the period of temporary vows, the nun may choose to take final or perpetual vows, committing herself for life to the monastic community. The ceremony for taking final vows is a solemn and joyful occasion, often involving the entire community as well as the nun's family and friends. The final vows represent a lifelong commitment to God, to the community, and to the monastic way of life.

Engaging with the Outside World

While the primary focus of convent life is often inward, with an emphasis on prayer and contemplation, many nuns in the 21st century also engage actively with the outside world through outreach and service. This engagement can take many forms, from direct service to advocacy and social justice work.

Nuns have historically been involved in education, and this continues today, with many nuns teaching in schools or running educational programs. In addition to traditional academic subjects, these programs often include religious education and moral development, aiming to instil values of compassion, justice, and service in their students. Healthcare is another area where nuns continue to make a significant impact. Many nuns work as nurses, doctors, or administrators in hospitals and clinics, providing care to the sick and the vulnerable. Their work is often motivated by a deep sense of compassion and a commitment to upholding the dignity of every human being. Advocacy and social justice work have also become increasingly important aspects of monastic life. Many nuns are involved in campaigns for human rights, environmental protection, and social equity. Whether through direct action, such as participating in protests or lobbying for policy change, or through more subtle forms of advocacy, such as educating the public or supporting grassroots movements, nuns are using their voices to speak out on issues that align with their spiritual values.

The Challenges of Modern Monastic Life

While the life of a nun in the 21st century is deeply fulfilling for many, it is not without its challenges. The decline in religious vocations, particularly in Europe and North America, has led to smaller communities and, in some cases, the closure of convents. This decline has placed additional responsibilities on the remaining nuns, who must take on multiple roles within the community.

Financial sustainability is another significant challenge. Many convents rely on income from their work or donations from supporters, but as the number of nuns decreases, so too does the ability to generate income. Some communities have adapted by diversifying their sources of income, such as by opening retreat centres or offering spiritual direction to laypeople. Another challenge is the tension between maintaining traditional monastic practices and adapting to the modern world. Some communities have embraced change, incorporating new technologies or more flexible forms of community life, while others have chosen to adhere strictly to their traditional practices. Balancing these demands requires careful discernment and a deep commitment to the core values of monastic life.

Chapter 8:

Celebrations and Calendar Events

The liturgical calendar and religious celebrations play a central role in the life of nuns, providing structure, rhythm, and a deep sense of connection to the broader Christian tradition. These events are not only times of worship and community but also opportunities for spiritual renewal, reflection, and growth. This chapter explores the most important celebrations and calendar events that shape the lives of nuns, highlighting their significance and the ways in which they are observed within convents.

The Liturgical Year

The life of a nun is deeply intertwined with the liturgical year, a cycle of seasons and feasts that marks the passage of time in the Christian tradition. The liturgical year begins with Advent, continues through Christmas, Lent, Easter, and Ordinary Time, and culminates in the Feast of Christ the King. Each season and feast within this cycle has its own spiritual significance and is observed with specific rituals, prayers, and customs.

Advent marks the beginning of the liturgical year and is a season of preparation and anticipation. For nuns, Advent is a time of reflection on the coming of Christ, both in the historical sense at Christmas and in the eschatological sense at the end of time. The four weeks of Advent are marked by special prayers, scripture readings, and the lighting of the Advent wreath, with each candle representing hope, peace, joy, and love. Nuns may also engage in additional acts of charity and fasting during this season as a way to prepare their hearts for the celebration of Christmas.

Christmas is one of the most joyous and significant celebrations in the liturgical year, marking the birth of Jesus Christ. The Christmas season begins on December 25th and lasts until the Feast of the Baptism of the Lord in early January. In convents, Christmas is celebrated with great reverence and joy, beginning with Midnight Mass on Christmas Eve, which is often a highlight of the season. The convent chapel is typically adorned with festive decorations, including a Nativity scene, and the nuns gather to sing carols, exchange greetings, and share a festive meal. The spirit of Christmas continues throughout the season, with daily prayers and readings focusing on the mystery of the Incarnation.

Lent is a penitential season that begins on Ash Wednesday and lasts for 40 days, leading up to Easter. It is a time of fasting, prayer, and almsgiving, during which nuns seek to deepen their spiritual lives through acts of penance and self-denial. The observance of Lent in convents includes additional periods of silence, the practice of the Stations of the Cross, and participation in communal penance services. Nuns may also take on personal Lenten disciplines, such as giving up certain foods or activities, as a way of drawing closer to God.

Holy Week, the final week of Lent, is the most solemn period of the liturgical year, commemorating the Passion, Death, and Resurrection of Jesus Christ. The week begins with Palm Sunday, which recalls Jesus' triumphant entry into Jerusalem. Nuns participate in the blessing and procession of palms, followed by the reading of the Passion narrative. The events of Holy Week culminate in the Triduum, the three days of Maundy Thursday, Good Friday, and Holy Saturday. These days are observed with special liturgies and devotions, including the Mass of the Lord's Supper on Maundy Thursday, the veneration of the Cross on Good Friday, and the Easter Vigil on Holy Saturday night.

Easter, the celebration of the Resurrection of Jesus, is the most important feast in the Christian calendar. The Easter season lasts for 50 days, from Easter Sunday to Pentecost. In convents, Easter is a time of great rejoicing, marked by the singing of the "Alleluia," the lighting of the Paschal candle, and the renewal of baptismal vows. The joy of Easter permeates the daily life of the convent, with festive meals, music, and decorations reflecting the triumph of life over death. The season concludes with the Feast of Pentecost, which commemorates the descent of the Holy Spirit upon the apostles and the birth of the Church.

Ordinary Time is the longest season in the liturgical year, encompassing the weeks outside the major seasons of Advent, Christmas, Lent, and Easter. Despite its name, Ordinary Time is not "ordinary" in the sense of being mundane; rather, it is a time for nuns to grow in their faith and deepen their spiritual lives through daily prayer, reflection, and service. The liturgies during this season focus on the teachings and miracles of Jesus, providing a continuous reflection on the Christian life.

Major Feast Days and Solemnities

In addition to the seasons of the liturgical year, there are specific feast days and solemnities that hold particular importance for nuns. These celebrations honour key events in the life of Jesus, the Virgin Mary, and the saints, and they are often marked by special liturgies, devotions, and communal celebrations.

The Feast of the Presentation of the Lord, also known as Candlemas, is celebrated on February 2nd and marks the presentation of Jesus in the Temple. In many convents, this day is observed with a candlelight procession, symbolizing Christ as the light of the world. The nuns may renew their commitment to their monastic vows on this day, reflecting on their own dedication to the light of Christ.

The Annunciation, celebrated on March 25th, commemorates the angel Gabriel's announcement to the Virgin Mary that she would conceive and bear the Son of

God. This feast is particularly significant in convents dedicated to Mary, and it is often marked by special prayers and reflections on Mary's role in salvation history.

The Feast of the Assumption of the Blessed Virgin Mary on August 15th is another major Marian celebration, honouring the belief that Mary was assumed body and soul into heaven. This feast is typically observed with a solemn Mass, processions, and devotions to Mary, and it is a day of great joy and celebration in many convents.

All Saints' Day, celebrated on November 1st, is a solemnity that honours all the saints, known and unknown. This feast is significant for nuns as a reminder of the communion of saints and the call to holiness. The day is marked by a festive Mass, prayers for the intercession of the saints, and a reflection on the lives of those who have gone before in faith.

The Feast of St. Benedict, celebrated on July 11th, is particularly important for Benedictine communities. St. Benedict is considered the father of Western monasticism, and his Rule continues to guide many monastic communities today. The feast is typically marked by a solemn Mass, readings from the Rule of St. Benedict, and a reflection on his legacy.

Celebrations of Profession and Jubilee

In addition to the liturgical celebrations, convents also observe special events that mark key moments in the lives of individual nuns and the community as a whole. Two of the most significant of these events are the profession of vows and the celebration of jubilees.

The Profession of Vows is a deeply significant event in the life of a nun. Whether it is the profession of temporary vows or final vows, this ceremony is a public commitment to the monastic life. The profession ceremony typically takes place within a solemn Mass, where the nun makes her vows of poverty, chastity, and obedience before the community and the presiding clergy. The ceremony may include the presentation of a religious habit, a ring, or other symbols of commitment, and it is often followed by a communal celebration.

Jubilee Celebrations mark significant anniversaries of a nun's profession of vows, such as 25, 50, or 60 years of religious life. These jubilees are times of joy and gratitude, celebrating the nun's long and faithful service to God and the community. The jubilee Mass is often a highlight of the celebration, with special prayers, readings, and blessings. The jubilee is also an occasion for the entire community to come together in a spirit of thanksgiving, often followed by a festive meal and other expressions of celebration.

Pilgrimages and Retreats

Pilgrimages and retreats are important practices in the spiritual life of many nuns, offering opportunities for renewal, reflection, and deepening of faith. While these events may not occur annually, they hold significant spiritual value and are eagerly anticipated by those who participate.

Pilgrimages are journeys to holy sites, undertaken as acts of devotion and spiritual seeking. For nuns, pilgrimages can be a powerful way to connect with the broader Christian tradition and to experience the universal church. Popular pilgrimage destinations include the Holy Land, Rome, Lourdes, and Santiago de Compostela. During a pilgrimage, nuns engage in prayer, reflection, and acts of penance, seeking spiritual growth and a deeper connection with God.

Retreats are times set aside for focused prayer, silence, and contemplation. While nuns already live a life oriented toward prayer, retreats offer an opportunity to withdraw even further from daily responsibilities and distractions. Retreats may be held within the convent or at a retreat centre, and they often include guided meditations, spiritual direction, and extended periods of silence. These retreats are vital for spiritual renewal, allowing nuns to reflect deeply on their vocation and their relationship with God.

The Role of Community in Celebrations

In the life of a nun, celebrations and calendar events are not just individual observances but are deeply communal experiences. The entire community comes together to mark these occasions, reinforcing the bonds of sisterhood and shared commitment to the monastic life.

The communal aspect of these celebrations is reflected in the shared liturgies, meals, and rituals that define convent life. Whether it is a major feast day, a profession ceremony, or a simple daily prayer, the presence and participation of the entire community are essential. These communal celebrations serve as reminders of the unity and solidarity that are at the heart of monastic life.

Chapter 9:

Statistical Overview of Monastic Life

In recent years, the number of women choosing to enter monastic life has seen significant changes, reflecting broader societal trends and the evolving role of religion in the modern world. This chapter provides a statistical overview of the trends in female monasticism, examining the percentage of women who become nuns, how many remain in the convent for life, and other relevant statistics that shed light on the dynamics of religious life for women today.

Percentage of Women Who Become Nuns

The decision to enter monastic life is a significant and often life-altering choice. However, it is a path that relatively few women choose in contemporary society. The percentage of women who become nuns varies by region, religious tradition, and socio-economic context.

Globally, the number of women entering convents has declined over the past several decades, particularly in Western countries. For example, in the United States, the number of women religious (nuns and sisters) peaked in the 1960s at around 180,000. By 2020, this number had decreased to approximately 42,000, representing a decline of over 75%. The percentage of Catholic women in the U.S.

who choose to enter religious life today is estimated to be less than 0.1%.

In Europe, the trend is similar, with many countries experiencing significant declines in the number of new entrants to convents. For example, in France, the number of women entering religious life has dropped by more than 60% since the 1960s. In Italy, where monasticism has a long and rich tradition, the number of new vocations has also decreased, though not as sharply as in some other European countries. In contrast, in some regions of Africa and Asia, the number of women entering religious life has remained stable or even increased. In countries like India and the Philippines, Catholicism continues to play a central role in society, and religious vocations are more common. For instance, in India, there are an estimated 90,000 Catholic nuns, and the number of women joining religious orders has remained relatively steady, particularly in rural areas where traditional religious values are more deeply ingrained.

Nuns Who Remain in Religious Life

Once a woman enters a convent, the path to taking final vows and remaining in religious life for the rest of her life can be challenging. The percentage of women who remain in religious life varies based on several factors, including the initial formation process, the support of the religious community, and the individual's personal discernment.

Studies have shown that a significant percentage of women who enter religious life do not take final vows. According to data from the National Religious Vocation Conference in the United States, about 20-30% of women who enter religious life leave before taking final vows. This attrition can occur for various reasons, including the realization that monastic life is not the right path for them, a desire to return to secular life, or personal and family reasons. Among those who do take final vows, the majority remain in religious life for the rest of their lives. For example, in the U.S., approximately 70-80% of women who take final vows continue in religious life until their death. This high retention rate reflects the deep commitment and strong sense of vocation among those who have fully embraced monastic life.

Celibacy and Abstinence

One of the defining aspects of monastic life is the vow of chastity, which includes a commitment to lifelong celibacy and abstinence from sexual activity. This vow is central to the spiritual life of nuns and is seen as a way of dedicating oneself entirely to God, free from the attachments of romantic or sexual relationships.

The vast majority of nuns who take final vows adhere strictly to this vow of celibacy. Instances of nuns leaving religious life to marry or engage in romantic relationships are relatively rare, though they do occur. When such situations arise, they often receive significant attention due to the perceived contradiction between the vow of chastity and the choice to enter into a sexual relationship. There is limited formal data on the exact percentage of nuns who remain celibate throughout their lives, as this is generally assumed to be the case for those who remain in religious life. However, anecdotal evidence and reports suggest that violations of the vow of chastity are infrequent, and the commitment to celibacy remains strong among those who have taken final vows.

Age and Demographics of Nuns

The age profile of nuns has shifted significantly over the past several decades, particularly in Western countries where the number of new entrants has declined. Today, the majority of nuns in countries like the United States, Canada, and Western Europe are over the age of 60. In the U.S., for example, nearly 80% of nuns are aged 60 or older, with a significant portion in their 70s and 80s.

This aging population of nuns presents challenges for religious communities, including issues related to healthcare, the sustainability of convents, and the transmission of traditions to younger generations. In many cases, convents have had to adapt by merging communities, selling off property, or finding new ways to support aging members. In contrast, in regions like Africa and Asia, where religious vocations remain more common, the age profile of nuns tends to be younger. In these regions, it is not uncommon to find a more balanced distribution of ages within religious communities, with younger women joining alongside older, more experienced nuns.

Educational Background and Roles

The educational background of nuns has evolved significantly, particularly in the 20th and 21st centuries. Historically, many women who entered convents did so with limited formal education, particularly in rural areas or in times when access to education for women was restricted. However, today, many nuns enter religious life with higher levels of education, including university degrees.

In fact, in some countries, a significant percentage of women who join religious orders have completed higher education before entering the convent. For example, in the United States, it is estimated that over 50% of women entering religious life today hold at least a bachelor's degree, and a growing number have advanced degrees in fields such as education, healthcare, theology, and social work. This higher level of education has allowed nuns to take on more specialized roles within their communities and in their work outside the convent. Many nuns serve as educators, healthcare professionals, social workers, and administrators, bringing their expertise to bear in ways that benefit both their religious communities and the broader society.

Vocational Trends

The trends in female monasticism are not uniform across the globe, reflecting the diverse cultural, social, and religious contexts in which nuns live and work. In Western countries, the decline in religious vocations has been linked to broader societal shifts, including the rise of secularism, greater opportunities for women in secular careers, and changing attitudes toward traditional religious practices.

In contrast, in parts of Africa, Asia, and Latin America, where Catholicism and other Christian denominations continue to play a central role in society, religious vocations remain more robust. In these regions, the decision to enter religious life is often supported by strong family and community ties, as well as a deep sense of religious duty. In countries like Nigeria, the Philippines, and Vietnam, the number of women entering religious life has remained relatively stable or even increased in recent years. These regions often serve as sources of new vocations for religious communities in the West, with nuns from these countries being sent to convents in Europe and North America to help sustain aging communities.

The Oldest Recorded Nun

The title of the oldest recorded nun in history is often attributed to Sister André (Lucile Randon), a French nun who lived to be 118 years old. Born on February 11, 1904, in Alès, France, she was baptized in the Protestant faith but converted to Catholicism at the age of 19. She joined the religious life in 1944, at the age of 40, becoming a member of the Daughters of Charity, a Catholic order known for its charitable works.

Sister André spent much of her life working as a governess, teacher, and later in a hospital, serving the poor and the sick. Even in her later years, Sister André remained an active and beloved member of her religious community. She became well-known internationally for her longevity and was recognized as the world's oldest living person by the Gerontology Research Group and Guinness World Records until her death on January 17, 2023, at the age of 118 years and 340 days.

The Oldest Living Nun

As of now, the title of the oldest living nun is not as widely reported or centralized, but Sister André was recognized as the oldest living nun before her death in 2023. After her passing, specific records about the current oldest living nun are not widely publicized, as the documentation of such records can be less formalized within religious communities compared to secular recognition of supercentenarians.

However, within various religious orders, there are often elderly nuns who have lived well into their 100s, continuing to serve or live within their communities. The longevity of these women is often celebrated within their orders but might not receive the same global attention unless they reach extraordinary ages like Sister André.

Notable Mentions

Sister Cecilia Maria (Marie Cecile Rey) was also a notably long-lived nun. Born in 1902 and passing away in 2018 at the age of 115, she was a French nun who, like Sister André, dedicated her life to service and charity.

Mother Cecilia of Jesus (Cecilia Requena Romero), a nun in Peru, reached 110 years before her passing in 2014. Her life was also marked by deep religious devotion and service.

While these are some of the most notable examples, many nuns have lived well into their 90s and 100s, a testament to their often healthy and disciplined lifestyles, spiritual fulfillment, and strong community support.

These women are remembered not only for their longevity but also for their unwavering dedication to their faith and the communities they served throughout their long lives.

Chapter 10:

Nuns in Hollywood: Reverence to Horror

Nuns have long been figures of fascination in popular culture, appearing in various forms of media, including literature, film, television, and art. Their representation in these mediums has ranged from depictions of piety and self-sacrifice to more complex and often sensationalized portrayals, particularly in the horror genre. This chapter explores how nuns are depicted in the media, with a particular focus on Hollywood films, and examines why the image of the nun has become so prominent in horror movies.

Nuns in Popular Media

The portrayal of nuns in popular media has evolved significantly over the years, reflecting broader societal attitudes toward religion, gender, and authority. In literature and early cinema, nuns were often depicted as paragons of virtue and selflessness, embodying ideals of piety, compassion, and service. These portrayals were influenced by the real-life roles that nuns played in education, healthcare, and social services, roles that were widely respected and admired.

One of the most iconic representations of nuns in media is the 1965 film *The Sound of Music*. Based on the true story of

Maria von Trapp, a young postulant who leaves the convent to become a governess, the film portrays the nuns of Nonnberg Abbey as kind, supportive, and nurturing. Their role in helping the von Trapp family escape the Nazis underscores the image of nuns as protectors and moral guides. *The Sound of Music* has remained a beloved classic, and its depiction of nuns has contributed to the popular image of religious women as gentle and selfless caregivers.

Similarly, films like *The Bells of St. Mary's* (1945) and *The Nun's Story* (1959) portray nuns in a positive light, emphasizing their dedication to service and their struggles with personal sacrifice and obedience. *The Nun's Story*, starring Audrey Hepburn, is particularly notable for its exploration of the internal conflicts faced by nuns, as it follows the journey of Sister Luke, who grapples with her vows and her desire to serve as a missionary nurse. The film highlights the complexities of monastic life and the challenges of balancing personal desires with religious commitment. However, as the 20th century progressed, the representation of nuns in media became more varied and, at times, controversial. Films like *Agnes of God* (1985), which deals with themes of mental illness, faith, and mystery, present nuns in more ambiguous and complex roles, reflecting a growing interest in the psychological and spiritual dimensions of religious life. The film's exploration of a young nun accused of infanticide raises questions about faith, innocence, and the darker aspects of religious life, challenging the more idealized portrayals of earlier films.

Television series have also contributed to the portrayal of nuns in popular culture. Shows like *Call the Midwife*, a British series based on the memoirs of a nurse midwife in London's East End in the 1950s and 60s, depict nuns as integral members of the community who provide healthcare and support to the poor. The series highlights the nuns' compassion, dedication, and resilience, while also exploring the challenges they face in a rapidly changing society.

Nuns in Horror Films

While nuns have been portrayed in various genres, their presence in horror films is particularly notable. The image of the nun in horror has become a recurring motif, often used to evoke fear, suspense, and unease. This portrayal contrasts sharply with the traditional image of nuns as figures of piety and virtue, raising questions about why nuns have become such popular characters in horror cinema.

One of the earliest examples of nuns in horror is the 1947 film *Black Narcissus*, which, while not a horror movie in the traditional sense, contains elements of psychological horror. The film tells the story of a group of Anglican nuns who struggle with isolation, desire, and madness while running a convent in the remote Himalayas. The intense atmosphere, combined with the nuns' internal conflicts and the exotic setting, creates a sense of psychological tension that borders on horror. It was not until the late 20th and early 21st centuries that nuns became central figures in horror films.

The 1970s saw the emergence of "nunsploitation" films, a subgenre of exploitation cinema that often depicted nuns in sensational and scandalous ways. Films like *The Devils* (1971) and *School of the Holy Beast* (1974) exploited the contrast between the sacred and the profane, using nuns as symbols of repressed desire and hidden sin. These films often combined elements of horror, eroticism, and religious critique, reflecting broader societal anxieties about religion, authority, and morality.

The trend of portraying nuns in horror continued into the 21st century, with films like *The Nun* (2018), a spin-off of *The Conjuring* series, which features a demonic nun as the central antagonist. *The Nun* capitalizes on the inherent eeriness of the nun's habit—its stark, uniform appearance and the way it obscures the wearer's identity—to create a sense of otherworldly dread. The film plays on the idea of the sacred being corrupted, with the demonic nun representing the ultimate perversion of religious purity.

Why Horror Loves Nuns

The frequent depiction of nuns in horror films can be attributed to several psychological and cultural factors. First, nuns are often seen as symbols of purity, chastity, and piety—qualities that, when subverted or corrupted, create a powerful sense of unease. The contrast between the expected sanctity of a nun and the horror of evil or supernatural forces creates a compelling narrative tension that filmmakers exploit to heighten fear and suspense. The image of the nun is also deeply tied to the concept of the "unseen" or "unknown," which is a common theme in horror. The nun's habit, which conceals her body and, in some cases, much of her face, adds to the sense of mystery and ambiguity. This visual obscurity allows for the projection of fears and anxieties onto the figure of the nun, making her an ideal vessel for horror's exploration of the unknown.

Additionally, horror films often delve into themes of guilt, sin, and punishment—concepts that are closely associated with religious life, particularly in the Catholic tradition. Nuns, as figures who are dedicated to a life of strict moral discipline, become natural symbols in stories that explore the consequences of moral failings or the presence of evil. The tension between the ideals of religious life and the darker aspects of human nature provides fertile ground for horror narratives.

Culturally, the portrayal of nuns in horror films can also be seen as a reflection of broader societal tensions with religion. In a world where traditional religious authority is increasingly questioned or rejected, the figure of the nun—who represents a life of strict adherence to religious doctrine—can be both fascinating and unsettling. Horror films that feature nuns often play on these tensions, using the figure of the nun to explore fears related to religious hypocrisy, repressed desires, or the supernatural.

The Impact of These Portrayals

The portrayal of nuns in horror films and other media has a significant impact on public perception, shaping how people view religious life and those who choose to dedicate themselves to it. While positive portrayals, such as those in *The Sound of Music* or *Call the Midwife*, reinforce the image of nuns as compassionate and selfless caregivers, the prevalence of nuns in horror films has introduced a more complex and sometimes negative image.

The association of nuns with horror and the supernatural can contribute to misconceptions about religious life, particularly for those who may have little direct experience with nuns or the monastic tradition. These portrayals can also reinforce stereotypes or fears about Catholicism and religious devotion, especially when they emphasize themes of repression, punishment, or corruption.

It's important to recognize that horror films, by their nature, are meant to explore the darker aspects of human experience. The use of nuns in these films often serves as a narrative device to heighten tension and evoke fear, rather than as a commentary on religious life itself. Nevertheless, the lasting impact of these portrayals on public perception cannot be overlooked, as they contribute to the broader cultural understanding of nuns and monastic life.

Conclusion:

The Legacy of Female Monasticism

As we reach the conclusion of this exploration into the world of female monasticism, we are reminded of the profound and enduring impact that nuns have had on both religious life and the broader society. From the early days of Christian monasticism to the challenges and adaptations of the 21st century, the journey of these women has been marked by a remarkable balance of tradition and innovation, deep spirituality, and a commitment to service.

Nuns have been pillars of faith, education, healthcare, and social justice, often stepping into roles where others could not or would not go. Their contributions have been diverse—ranging from the quiet, contemplative life of prayer and reflection to the active engagement in global issues such as human rights, environmental stewardship, and the fight against poverty. Each chapter of their history is a testament to their resilience, creativity, and unwavering dedication to their calling.

In the modern world, where religious vocations are declining in many parts of the globe, the story of nuns is not one of retreat but of transformation. They have embraced new challenges with the same spirit that guided their predecessors, finding ways to remain relevant and impactful in a rapidly changing society. Whether through the use of technology, new forms of community life, or deepening their involvement in social justice issues, nuns continue to adapt and thrive. The cultural representation of nuns in media and popular culture further underscores their significance, even if these portrayals sometimes contrast sharply with the reality of monastic life. From the reverent depictions of their selfless service to the more complex and often sensationalized portrayals in horror films, nuns remain figures of fascination, embodying both the sacred and the mysterious.

As we have seen, the life of a nun is one of profound commitment—marked by the vows of poverty, chastity, and obedience, and guided by the rhythms of prayer, work, and community. This life is not without its challenges, but it is also filled with deep meaning and purpose. Nuns have shown that a life dedicated to faith and service can be both fulfilling and transformative, not only for themselves but for the countless individuals and communities they have touched. The legacy of female monasticism is one of enduring influence—a legacy that continues to inspire, challenge, and uplift. As we move forward into an uncertain future, the example of these women serves as a powerful reminder of the strength of faith, the importance of community, and the lasting impact of a life lived in service to others.

In conclusion, the story of nuns is far from over. It is a story that continues to be written, shaped by the women who choose to dedicate their lives to this ancient yet ever-relevant way of life. Their journey is one of faith, resilience, and hope—a journey that will undoubtedly continue to inspire generations to come.

Notable Nuns in History:

St. Brigid of Kildare (c. 451–525)

Irish abbess; one of Ireland's patron saints; founder of several monasteries, including Kildare Abbey.

St. Scholastica (c. 480–543)

Twin sister of St. Benedict of Nursia; founder of a religious order for women; regarded as the patron saint of nuns.

St. Clare of Assisi (1194–1253)

Italian nun; founder of the Order of Poor Ladies (Poor Clares); close associate of St. Francis of Assisi.

St. Hildegard of Bingen (1098–1179)

German Benedictine abbess, mystic, and polymath; influential in theology, medicine, and music; Doctor of the Church.

St. Elizabeth of Hungary (1207–1231)

Hungarian princess and member of the Third Order of St. Francis; known for her charity to the poor and the sick.

St. Catherine of Siena (1347–1380)

Italian Dominican tertiary and mystic; key figure in bringing the papacy back to Rome; Doctor of the Church.

St. Teresa of Ávila (1515–1582)

Spanish Carmelite nun, mystic, and theologian; reformer of the Carmelite Order; Doctor of the Church.

St. Rose of Lima (1586–1617)

Peruvian Dominican tertiary; the first person born in the Americas to be canonized; known for her life of severe asceticism and care for the poor.

Sister Juana Inés de la Cruz (1648–1695)

Mexican Hieronymite nun, scholar, and poet; a major literary figure of the Spanish Golden Age.

St. Bernadette Soubirous (1844–1879)

French nun; visionary of the Marian apparitions at Lourdes; canonized in 1933.

St. Mary MacKillop (St. Mary of the Cross) (1842–1909)

Australian nun; co-founder of the Sisters of St. Joseph of the Sacred Heart; canonized as Australia's first saint in 2010.

St. Thérèse of Lisieux (1873–1897)

French Carmelite nun known for her "Little Way" of spirituality; author of *The Story of a Soul*; Doctor of the Church.

St. Elizabeth Ann Seton (1774–1821)

First native-born American to be canonized; founder of the Sisters of Charity; pioneer in Catholic education in the United States.

Sister Blandina Segale (1850–1941)

Italian-American nun; missionary and educator in the American Southwest; known for her encounters with Billy the Kid and for advocating for Native American and Hispanic communities.

Sister Dorothy Stang (1931–2005)

American-born nun and martyr; advocate for land reform and environmental protection in the Brazilian Amazon; murdered for her activism.

Mother Teresa (St. Teresa of Calcutta) (1910–1997)

Albanian-Indian Roman Catholic nun and missionary; founder of the Missionaries of Charity; Nobel Peace Prize laureate; canonized in 2016.

Notable Living Nuns

(as of the time of publishing)

Sister Madonna Buder (b. 1930)

American Roman Catholic nun and triathlete; known as the "Iron Nun" for her participation in over 400 triathlons.

Sister Jeannine Gramick (b. 1942)

American Roman Catholic nun; co-founder of New Ways Ministry, which advocates for LGBTQ+ rights within the Catholic Church.

Sister Joan Chittister (b. 1936)

American Benedictine nun, theologian, and author; advocate for women's rights, peace, and justice.

Sister Helen Prejean (b. 1939)

American Sister of St. Joseph; prominent advocate for the abolition of the death penalty; author of *Dead Man Walking*.

Sister Simone Campbell (b. 1945)

American Sister of Social Service; executive director of NETWORK; leader of the "Nuns on the Bus" campaigns.

Sister Catherine Wybourne (b. 1954)

English Benedictine nun; known as the "Digital Nun" for her use of social media to engage with contemporary issues.

Sister Mary Scullion (b. 1953)

American nun; co-founder of Project HOME, an organization that provides housing and support services for homeless individuals in Philadelphia.

Sister Consuelo Morales (b. 1948)

Mexican nun and human rights activist; founder of Citizens in Support of Human Rights (CADHAC), which works to address human rights abuses in Mexico.

Sister Norma Pimentel (b. 1953)

Mexican-American nun; executive director of Catholic Charities of the Rio Grande Valley; advocate for immigrants and refugees.

Sister Teresa Forcades (b. 1966)

Spanish Benedictine nun; theologian, physician, and social activist known for her critiques of the pharmaceutical industry and her advocacy for social justice.

Sister Rosemary Nyirumbe (b. 1956)

Ugandan nun; member of the Sisters of the Sacred Heart of Jesus; known for her work with survivors of war and sexual violence in Uganda and South Sudan.

Sister Pat Farrell (b. 1944)

American Franciscan nun; former president of the Leadership Conference of Women Religious (LCWR); advocate for social justice and dialogue within the Church.

Sister Brigid McDonald (b. 1926)

American Sister of St. Joseph of Carondelet; activist known for her peace and justice work, including protests against nuclear weapons.

Bibliography

Chapter 1:
Early Beginnings (4th-9th Century)

1. McNamara, Jo Ann. *Sisters in Arms: Catholic Nuns Through Two Millennia.* Harvard University Press, 1996.
2. Coon, Lynda L. *Sacred Fictions: Holy Women and Hagiography in Late Antiquity.* University of Pennsylvania Press, 1997.
3. Clark, Elizabeth A. *Women in the Early Church.* Liturgical Press, 1983.

Chapter 2:
The Medieval Era (10th-15th Century)

1. Elliott, Dyan. *Proving Woman: Female Spirituality and Inquisitional Culture in the Later Middle Ages.* Princeton University Press, 2004.
2. McGinn, Bernard. *The Flowering of Mysticism: Men and Women in the New Mysticism (1200-1350).* Crossroad Publishing, 1998.
3. Bynum, Caroline Walker. *Holy Feast and Holy Fast: The Religious Significance of Food to Medieval Women.* University of California Press, 1987.
4. Bynum, Caroline Walker. *Fragmentation and Redemption: Essays on Gender and the Human Body in Medieval Religion.* Zone Books, 1991.

Chapter 3:
Renaissance and Reformation (15th-17th Century)

1. Bell, Rudolph M. *How to Do It: Guides to Good Living for Renaissance Italians.* University of Chicago Press, 1999.
2. Eire, Carlos M. N. *Reformations: The Early Modern World, 1450-1650.* Yale University Press, 2016.
3. Teresa of Ávila. *The Life of Saint Teresa of Ávila by Herself.* Translated by J.M. Cohen, Penguin Classics, 1957.

4. McNamara, Jo Ann. *Sisters in Arms: Catholic Nuns Through Two Millennia*. Harvard University Press, 1996.

Chapter 4:
From Enlightenment to Modernity (18th-20th Century)

1. Clark, Emily. *Masterless Mistresses: The New Orleans Ursulines and the Development of a New World Society, 1727-1834*. University of North Carolina Press, 2007.
2. Porterfield, Amanda. *Mary Lyon and the Mount Holyoke Missionaries*. Oxford University Press, 1997.
3. Schroeder, Sister Mary Peter. *American Catholic Women: A Historical Exploration*. Sheed & Ward, 1987.
4. McGuinness, Margaret M. *Called to Serve: A History of Nuns in America*. New York University Press, 2013.

Chapter 5:
Contemporary Nuns (20th-21st Century)

1. McGuinness, Margaret M. *Called to Serve: A History of Nuns in America*. New York University Press, 2013.
2. Sullivan, Elizabeth Teresa. *Nuns and Nunneries in Renaissance Florence*. Johns Hopkins University Press, 2016.
3. Wall, Barbara Mann. *Unlikely Entrepreneurs: Catholic Sisters and the Hospital Marketplace, 1865-1925*. Ohio State University Press, 2005.
4. Williams, Maria Patricia. *Women Religious History Sources: A Guide to Repositories in the United States*. Routledge, 1999.

Chapter 6:
Nuns in the Modern World

1. Kuhns, Elizabeth A. *The Habit: A History of the Clothing of Catholic Nuns*. Doubleday, 2003.
2. Johnson, Mary L. and Rouleau, Patricia Wittberg. *The Power of Sisterhood: Women Religious Tell the Story of the Apostolic Visitation*. University Press of America, 2012.

3. McNamara, Jo Ann. *Sisters in Arms: Catholic Nuns Through Two Millennia*. Harvard University Press, 1996.

Chapter 7:
Life and Rituals of Nuns in the 21st Century Convent

1. Schroeder, Sister Mary Peter. *American Catholic Women: A Historical Exploration*. Sheed & Ward, 1987.
2. Porter, Jean. *The Recovery of Virtue: The Relevance of Aquinas for Christian Ethics*. Westminster John Knox Press, 1990.
3. Griffith, R. Marie. *God's Daughters: Evangelical Women and the Power of Submission*. University of California Press, 1997.

Chapter 8:
Celebrations and Calendar Events in the Life of Nuns

1. Lanzetta, Beverly J. *Radical Wisdom: A Feminist Mystical Theology*. Fortress Press, 2005.
2. Hickey, William. *The Liturgy Documents, Volume One: Essential Documents for Parish Worship*. Liturgy Training Publications, 2012.
3. Weaver, Mary Jo. *New Catholic Women: A Contemporary Challenge to Traditional Religious Authority*. Indiana University Press, 1995.

Chapter 9:
Statistical Overview of Women in Monastic Life

1. Bugnini, Annibale. *The Reform of the Liturgy 1948-1975*. Liturgical Press, 1990.
2. Mitchell, Nathan D. *Meeting Mystery: Liturgy, Worship, Sacraments*. Orbis Books, 2006.
3. Leclercq, Jean. *The Love of Learning and the Desire for God: A Study of Monastic Culture*. Fordham University Press, 1982.

Chapter 10:
Nuns in Media and Hollywood: From Reverence to Horror

1. Kennedy, Thomas C. *The Catholic Church in the Twentieth-Century America: An Overview.* University of Chicago Press, 2005.
2. Vatican Statistical Yearbook (Annuarium Statisticum Ecclesiae). Vatican Press.
3. Chinnici, Joseph P. *Living Stones: The History and Structure of Catholic Spiritual Life in the United States.* Crossroad Publishing, 1996.

Printed in Great Britain
by Amazon